When My Dad Lost His Job

KIDS HAVE *TROUBLES* TOO

When My Dad
Lost His Job

by Sheila Stewart and Rae Simons

Mason Crest Publishers

MASON CREST PUBLISHERS INC.
370 Reed Road
Broomall, Pennsylvania 19008
(866)MCP-BOOK (toll free)
www.masoncrest.com

First Printing
9 8 7 6 5 4 3 2 1

Library of Congress Cataloging-in-Publication Data

Stewart, Sheila, 1975–
 When my dad lost his job / by Sheila Stewart and Rae Simons.
    p. cm.
 Includes index.
  ISBN (set) 978-1-4222-1691-0   ISBN 978-1-4222-1703-0
  ISBN (ppbk set) 978-1-4222-1904-1   ISBN 978-1-4222-1916-4 (pbk)
 1. Unemployed—Juvenile literature. 2. Children of unemployed parents—Juvenile literature. I. Simons, Rae, 1957- II. Title.
  HD5707.5S74 2011
  305.9'0694—dc22
                                        2010029700
Design by MK Bassett-Harvey.
Produced by Harding House Publishing Service, Inc.
www.hardinghousepages.com
Illustrations by Russell Richardson, RxDx Productions.
Cover design by Torque Advertising + Design.
Printed in USA by Bang Printing.

The creators of this book have made every effort to provide accurate information, but it should not be used as a substitute for the help and services of trained professionals.

Introduction

Each child is unique—and each child encounters a unique set of circumstances in life. Some of these circumstances are more challenging than others, and how a child copes with those challenges will depend in large part on the other resources in her life.

The issues children encounter cover a wide range. Some of these are common to almost all children, including threats to self-esteem, anger management, and learning to identify emotions. Others are more unique to individual families, but problems such as parental unemployment, a death in the family, or divorce and remarriage are common but traumatic events in many children's lives. Still others—like domestic abuse, alcoholism, and the incarceration of a family member—are unfortunately not uncommon in today's world.

Whatever problems a child encounters in life, understanding that he is not alone is a key component to helping him cope. These books, both their fiction and nonfiction elements, allow children to see that other children are in the same situations. The books make excellent tools for triggering conversation in a nonthreatening way. They will also promote understanding and compassion in children who may not be experiencing these issues themselves.

These books offer children important factual information—but perhaps more important, they offer hope.

—*Cindy Croft, M.A., Ed., Director of the Center for Inclusive Child Care*

It all started in September, the first week of school. When I got home that day, my dad was just sitting at the kitchen table looking angry. My mom was standing behind him with tears on her face. I threw my backpack on the floor, and opened my mouth, ready to tell them about my day at school, but then it sunk in—my dad shouldn't be home from work yet, and the expression on their faces told me something bad had happened.

I just stood there in the doorway, too scared to say anything. I thought maybe something had happened to Grandma or Grandpa.

But that wasn't what it was.

My parents looked up at me, but it took them a couple of seconds, as though for just an instant there, they'd been too upset to even notice me. It's a weird feeling when your parents think you're invisible, but it's been happening a lot the last few months. I don't like it.

"What happened?" I managed to say. "How come Dad's home from work?" I pretended I hadn't noticed that Mom was crying. I guess I thought I could make it not be true.

Mom wiped her face. "Your dad lost his job, Kayley."

"Oh." That seemed a lot better than something being wrong with Grandma or Grandpa. I didn't really understand then why his losing his job was so bad. I sat down at the table across from my dad.

"So," I said after a couple of seconds, "can't you get another job?"

Dad looked up at me, and he didn't look angry anymore, he just looked sad, like maybe he was going to cry too. That made me feel scared all over again. Sometimes Dad would cry over sad movies and that would make Mom laugh, but he didn't usually cry about other stuff.

"I don't think I'm going to be able to get another job, Kayley," he said. "Not for a while. At least not one where I'll make the kind of money we're used to me making."

I slid the salt and pepper shakers back and forth across the table. "Well, Mom's still got her job, right?"

My mother is a teacher's aide at the elementary school, but she only works part time, so she can be back home by the time I get off the bus.

"Yes, I still have my job," Mom said. She sat down at the table next to Dad, and the three of us sat there looking at each other. "I've already asked for extra hours, and I'll start working full time next week."

I tried out a smile. "Well, that's good."

"I won't be here anymore when you get home from school." Mom looked really sad about this, so I made my smile bigger.

"That's okay. I'm ten years old, Mom. I can manage on my own after school."

"Well," Dad said, "for now, I'll be at home when you get off the bus."

I still wasn't getting why this was upsetting them so much. It really didn't sound like the end of the world to me. Dad had been complaining about his job a lot lately. It seemed to me like he might be happy to have a break from it.

And that night, my parents seemed to shake off their sad feelings and go back to normal. Mom looked through my homework with me, while Dad got supper. We ate, watched some television, went to bed, and I stopped worrying about it.

I didn't realize then all the changes that were coming. Not only did Mom start working full time at school, but she also got a job in the evenings working at a grocery store on the other side of town. She didn't get home until after I was in bed, so I only saw her for about a half hour in the mornings before I went to school. Then we'd see each other on Saturdays and Sundays, until four in the afternoon, when she had to go to work at the grocery store.

Meanwhile, Dad was home all the time. He was waiting for his unemployment checks to start, and he was looking for work while I was at school, but so far he hadn't found anything. At first, it was kind of fun to have Dad around so much. He'd do crazy things like have a water fight with me in the kitchen or make me laugh while I was doing my homework.

But I missed Mom. And more and more, Dad just wanted to sit and stare at the television or play his guitar. He started doing that thing a lot where I

felt like he really couldn't see me anymore, like I'd turned invisible.

And when he did see me, he was grouchy most of the time. He'd snap at me over little things that would never have bothered Mom, like me leaving my schoolwork spread out on the floor in the living room.

And then there was the day I forgot to feed the cat before I went to school. I walked in the door after school and found Cattie yowling and Dad stomping around muttering.

"What is wrong with the cat?" he snapped at me. "She's been driving me crazy all day. Why can't she be quiet? If she can't shut up, I'm going to put her out in the garage."

I bent down and pet Cattie's soft gray fur. She rubbed against my legs and then ran to her empty food dish. "Meow?" she said, that little squeaky sound she makes that sounds like a question. "MEOW?" she said louder.

"See?" Dad said. "She's given me a headache."

"Dad," I said, thinking he was being kind of stupid because it was so obvious what was wrong with Cattie, "she's HUNGRY. She wants someone to feed her." I went to the cupboard and got out her cat food. Cattie immediately started purring loudly.

Dad glared at us both. "Well, then, Kayley, why didn't you feed her before you went to school? You know that's your job."

"I know," I said, as I put a handful of crunchy food in Cattie's bowl. "But I forgot."

Dad sighed. "Kayley, if I can't count on you to remember to do something as little as that, we've got a problem. Your mother and I need to know you're doing your part around here."

After spending days while Dad ignored me half the time and I tried not to bother him, I was pretty sure I HAD been doing my part. I missed Mom, and I missed Dad being in a good mood. And all of sudden it all just seemed like too much to bear.

Dad was glaring at me, and I glared right back at him. "I don't know what the big deal is," I said. "So I forgot. You could have just fed Cattie yourself. How hard would that have been? It's what Mom would have done. She wouldn't have made such a big thing about it."

Dad's face turned red, and I knew I had crossed a line I shouldn't have. "Kayley Moore, don't you dare speak to me like that!" His voice was getting louder and louder.

I just stood there, watching Cattie eat, trying not to cry, while he yelled at me.

"Do you understand?" he asked when he was finally done.

I nodded. And then I picked up Cattie and went to my room. I slammed my door shut behind me. "I hate you!" I whispered, but I wasn't talking to Cattie. Right then, I really felt like I hated my dad.

By this time, it was November, and I understood now why Mom and Dad had looked so upset that day back in September. Life just wasn't the same anymore. With Mom gone so much, the house felt weird. I couldn't wait till Saturdays and Sundays when I could see her, but she was always tired on her days off, and she and Dad fought a lot more than they ever had before. Some weekends I'd end up just hiding in my room, staying out of their way while they argued about bills and money and stuff I didn't understand. What was really scaring me now was a whole new worry—what if Mom and Dad didn't love each other anymore? What if they got a divorce?

I got sick with the flu a week before Thanksgiving, and it was terrible. Dad took me to the doctor, and he brought me drinks and soup—but he wasn't Mom. Mom would have sat beside my bed and read to me. She and I would have talked about when she was little and we would have watched movies together. We would have had a good time, even though I was sick.

Dad just stomped around looking grouchier than ever, making me feel guilty for being such a bother.

I got better finally—and by then it was Christmas time. Life started to seem a little better. It was already the middle of December, and we still didn't have a Christmas tree, but putting up the tree had always been Mom's and my job, and I knew Mom had been too busy and tired to get to it yet. But she was going to have an entire week and a half off from her job at the school, and she would also have a couple of days off from the grocery store. I couldn't wait.

But the Saturday before school got out for Christmas vacation, I got up to find Mom and Dad in the kitchen again, with the same upset looks on their faces they'd had on that day back in September when Dad lost his job.

"What now?" I asked them.

I knew they'd been arguing before I'd come in the kitchen, and now they were going through those few moments when they had to stretch their eyes back into a shape that was able to see their daughter again. Mom was the first one to really look at me. She wiped the tears off her face, just like she had last time, and then she put her arm around me.

"We're going to have to move," she said.

I didn't say anything. Dad was leaning against the kitchen counter, looking sad and angry. "We can't afford this house any longer, Kayley," he said. "I'm sorry. It was always a stretch for us to pay the mortgage, and now there's just no way we can keep doing it. We've tried everything we could think of, but there's no avoiding it any longer. Your mother and I have finally come to an agreement."

"Oh." I looked at them. "Is THAT what you've been fighting about?"

They looked at each other. "Mostly," Mom said.

I sucked in a deep breath, feeling kind of relieved. Then I waited for them to say something more, like maybe that we couldn't have any Christmas this year. Maybe there was NEVER going to be a Christmas tree this year.

When they didn't say anything else, I finally asked, "Where do we have to move?"

As I asked the question, my heart kind of sank. I've heard grownups say that, and now I knew what they meant. I felt like my heart was dropping down lower and lower inside my chest, as though it suddenly weighted about fifty pounds. "Do we have to move across the country?" I asked. "Will I have to go to a new school? Will I have to leave all my friends?"

"No, no," Mom said. "None of that. We just have to find a smaller place to live, somewhere cheaper. A lot cheaper."

"Oh." I thought about that. "You mean somewhere near here?"

Dad nodded. "Somewhere in town. We don't want your mom to lose her jobs. I'm applying for work all over the country, and if I get something somewhere else, then we'll need to talk about moving further. But not right now."

Not right now. I didn't like the sound of that but at least for now, it could have been worse. Another awful thought occurred to me, though.

"Will we be able to keep Cattie?"

Mom smiled at me. "Of course, Kayley. Cattie's part of the family. Where we go, she goes."

"Okay," I said again. And then I asked the other thing that had been bothering me. "We're still going to have Christmas?"

Mom and Dad looked at each other again, and this time they laughed. I knew they were kind of laughing at me, but I was so happy to see them look like they liked each other again that I didn't mind. "Yes, Kayley," Dad said. "We're still going to have Christmas."

"There won't be as many presents as other years, though" Mom said.

"But we'll have a Christmas tree? And bake cookies? And Grandma and Grandpa will come over?"

"Yes, yes, yes," Mom said, laughing. "We'll do all those things."

And we did. We also went house shopping, which I thought was fun, and we found a little house outside town to buy. I wouldn't be able to ride my bike to my friends' houses anymore, but Dad said I could ride the bus home with them sometimes, and then he'd pick me up.

What I liked best about the new house was that it had a big back yard with an apple tree I could climb. I'd always wanted to live in the country, and now we would.

We moved into the new house in February. It was too small to hold all our stuff from the big house, so we had a garage sale and sold lots of things. I helped

Dad set it up, and then I collected the cash from people. It was fun.

As we walked through the old house one last time, I noticed Mom was crying again, and even Dad had tears in his eyes.

"So what's the matter with you two now?" I asked, feeling scared that there was going to be more bad news.

"I love this house," Mom said. "Don't you?"

I looked around the empty house. We'd moved here from a smaller house a few blocks away when I was seven, and at the time, I remember how excited I was about living in such a huge house. But I'd started to hate living here the last few months. It just seemed big and lonely. Maybe I'd miss some things about it, but I didn't think so. It was only a house, after all.

"Nope," I said. "But I love YOU, Mom. And I love Cattie."

"What about me?" Dad looked kind of worried, and I knew he was thinking of all the times we'd argued over the past few weeks.

I grinned up at him. "I love you too, Dad. Even if you don't have a job. Even if we don't have as much money as we used to." I pulled my parents close together and hugged them both at the same time.

"So long as we're all together, that's all that matters."

What Job Loss Means

As a kid, it's hard to understand how big a deal losing your job can be. At first, Kayley didn't get why her parents were so upset, but as time went on, she realized how many changes it led to. Jobs are an important of part of adult life. You need a job to earn money to eat and to pay for your house or apartment. Having a job also means you're a **productive** member of society, and have something to do every day. Often, jobs are part of adults' identities. When they lose that job, they lose a part of who they are.

Your parents have to worry about having enough money to take care of you and your siblings, if you have any. Losing a job means losing the ability to do that, which is very scary. It's also hard to find another job. There aren't always jobs around, or there aren't jobs that your parent is **qualified** to fill. Your mom and dad might have spent years getting an education for whatever job they had before. They have lots of skills to

Understand the Word

If you're a **productive** member of society, it means that you contribute something to it. By having a job, you are useful and make the world a better place.

Being **qualified** for a job means that you have all the skills and requirements to do it well. You wouldn't be qualified to be a doctor, for example, if you had not attended medical school.

Many parents are happy to be able to work and earn money to provide for their families' needs.

do that job, but they may not have been trained to do other jobs. For example, if your dad was a teacher, he knows all about helping kids learn. He doesn't know about curing sick people, or fixing cars, so he has to look for a job where he can use his skills. Sometimes, he may have to settle for a job where he makes less money, because he can't find a job in the area where he's trained.

Understand the Word

When there are less of all the things that have to do with money in a country, including jobs and how many products the country produces, the country is said to be in **recession**. Recessions last at least six months.

Kids, on the other hand, are too busy with school and play and activities to worry too much about jobs. Even if you did have a part-time job delivering papers or babysitting, you probably wouldn't be too upset if you lost it. You don't have to take care of your parents with the money you earn now, and you could just get another job somewhere else. Try to look at it from your parents' point of view, though, and you might start to understand why they're so upset.

Job Loss Right Now

Job loss is an even more important issue than usual right now. There are always people losing jobs, but more people than ever are losing them in the past few years. Businesses all over the world are in trouble, and the world has entered a **recession**. Thousands of people have lost their jobs, and more are losing them every day. There are a lot of people without work, looking for new jobs. Every time one job opens up somewhere, lots of people compete for it, but only one person gets it. That makes losing your job even harder to cope with now.

A lot of people are looking for work, and the jobs aren't always available.

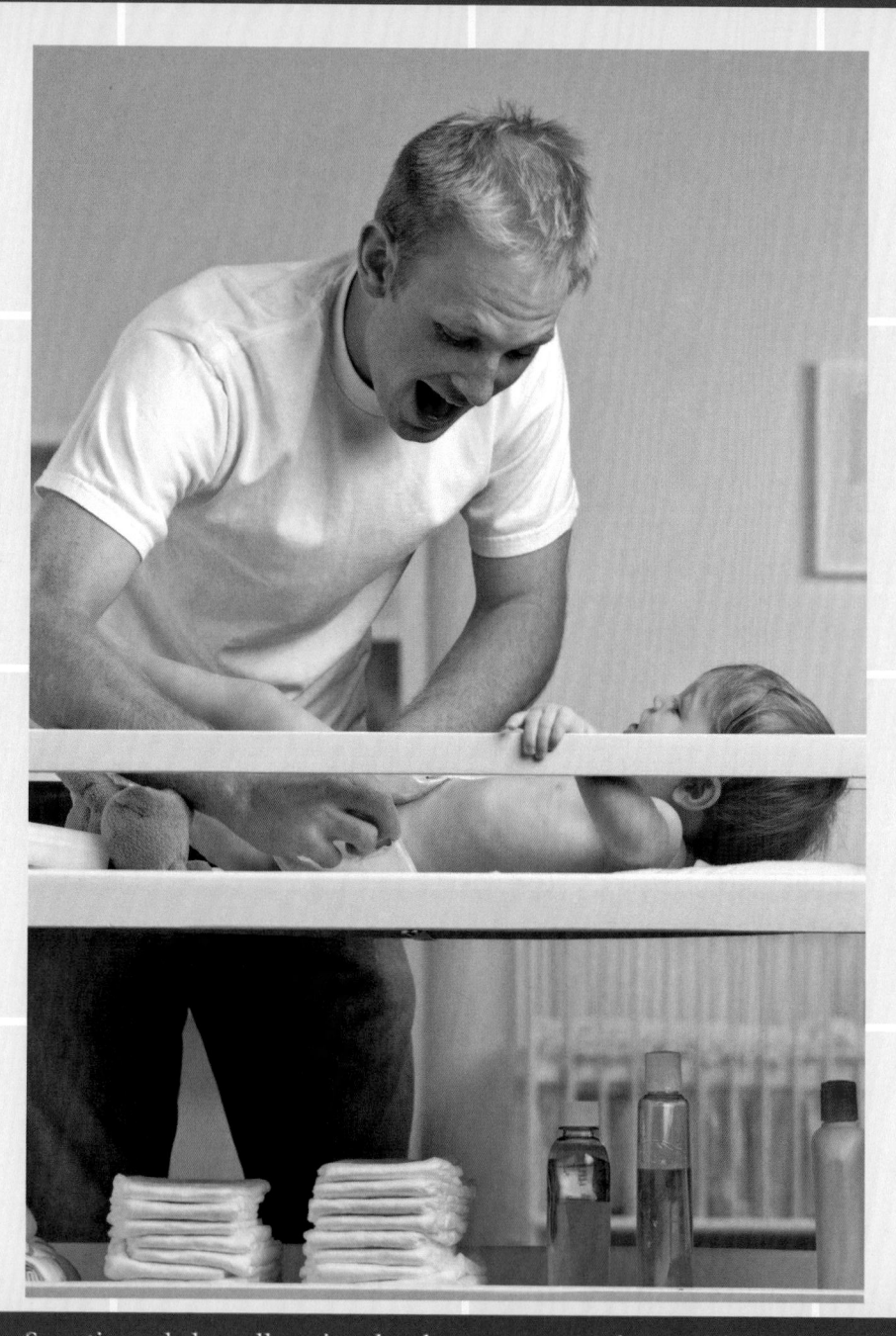

Sometimes dads really enjoy the chance to stay at home and spend time with their kids.

What Happens Next

Every family deals with job loss differently. Kayley's dad stayed home and looked for a job while her mom worked extra hours and took another job. Then they had to move because they couldn't afford their house. In other families where the dad loses his job, he might be happy to stay home and take care of the kids for a change, and he wouldn't bother to look for a job, but not many families these days can afford to live on one income for very long.

It used to be that only moms stayed home and took care of the house and kids while the dad worked, but these days, more and more fathers are doing that instead. So maybe if your dad loses his job and your mom still has a high-paying one, you'll get a stay-at-home dad.

Changes like these can make your family feel a little different. You won't see as much of the parent that used to stay home or work less, but you'll sure see a lot of the one who is out of work. It's almost like your parents switched! That can be a good and a bad thing. You get to spend time with the parent that you only saw on weekends or at night, but you also have to get used to a different way of doing things.

Sometimes when people lose jobs, they decide to go back to school to learn how to do something else. College isn't just for teenagers—lots of older people end up going back to college to get degrees in subjects that will help them get a new job. For example, jobs that have to do with computers are in demand right now, so your mom might consider getting a degree in computer science from the local community college so she can work for a company doing things with computers.

Your family might have to move to another town when your parent loses his or her job. This could mean moving across the state or across the country. Moving is hard, but you'll get used to your new home.

Making Sacrifices

Once your parent loses a job, your family will have less money. You'll have to learn to live without some of the things you're used to having. Eating out at restaurants, going to the movies, and buying new clothes all

the time cost a lot of money, and your parents probably can't afford to pay for those things right now. That
doesn't mean they never will, but right now, they're
too expensive.

You might even have to give up bigger things. Your
house could be too expensive or you might have to sell
a car. These sorts of things cost a lot of money, and
if your parents just don't have the **financial means**,
then you'll all have to live without them.

Keeping Order

Not everything has to change. Having a
parent that loses a job can create a lot of
chaos in your house, so you want to keep
as many things the same as possible. Even
if your dad is at home now instead of
your mom, try to keep the same schedule
you had before. If you have family game night every
Wednesday, or both your parents came to watch you
play baseball every Saturday afternoon, don't change
that now if you can help it. And definitely don't stop
celebrating special holidays, like Kayley was worried
her family would do!

> ### *Understand the Word*
>
> Taken together, your money, property, and other wealth are your **financial means**.

It can be hard to know what to do with the emotions you have about all the changes in your life.

Dealing with Feelings

You're probably going to feel a lot of different emotions if your mom or dad loses a job. Here's a list of some of the things you could feel:

- Confusion. You might not really understand what's going on, or why everyone is so upset.
- Anger. You might feel like it's your parents' fault. After all, it's your parents' job to take care of the family, and you could be angry that they don't seem to be doing that right. You could also be angry if you have to give up things that are important to you, like going skiing or another expensive activity—or if you have to leave your home or school.
- Worry. Anxiety and worry are common, especially if you don't know what's going to happen in the future. Will you be able to afford everything? Will you have to move? Will your parent find another job? No one likes the unknown!
- Frustration. You just want everything back the way it was, before the job loss, but there's nothing you can do to change the situation. You don't want to

have to deal with having a new parent at home, or going through the stress of moving.

• Stress. Suddenly you have to keep track of all your **expenses**, be more responsible at home, and deal with emotional parents. All of that can add up to a lot of stress for kids in the family.

Understand the Word

Expenses are anything you buy that costs money. Cars, houses, clothes, movies, health care, and toys are all different kinds of expenses.

Feeling any of these emotions is completely normal. Don't feel guilty if you have these feelings! It makes sense that you'll have some pretty extreme feelings, since this is an extreme situation. The important thing is to be in control of your emotions and not to let them take control of you. Don't take your anger and frustration out on your parents, siblings, or friends, and don't let yourself go crazy with stress. Instead, run around, dance to music, or write in a journal, anything to deal positively with your feelings. If you do vent your emotions on others— and we all make that mistake sometimes—be sure to say you're sorry. Talking with your family and friends

Writing about what's going on in your life and how you feel about it can be
a helpful way to deal with difficult experiences.

about what you're feeling will help you all understand each other better.

Keep Talking

Don't keep all your thoughts and feelings locked away inside, or they could erupt at any minute. There are

Talking to your Mom or Dad, or to another adult, is another good way to figure out how to deal with your emotions.

lots of people you can talk to instead, who can help you figure out the situation.

First, talking to your parents is very important. It will help to tell your parents how you're feeling, so that they can help you. If they don't know that you're upset, then they can't make you feel better. Together, you can come up with ways of dealing with your parent's job loss so that you're happier. You can even be part of the decisions having to do with how to spend money from now on, how to deal with one parent being home all the time, or where to move. In fact, holding family conferences is a good idea, so that everyone in your family gets their voice heard by everyone else, and you're all on the same page when dealing with the situation.

If you'd rather talk to someone outside of your family, try talking to a trusted teacher, family friend, coach, or other adult. A great person to go to is your school counselor. Counselors are people who work at schools, who have been trained to listen to students' problems and help them figure out how to solve them. They can help you with anything from issues with friends, to a death in the family, to a parent losing a job.

You might even discover that your friends have gone through the same experience as you, or are going through it right now. Lots of families have parents that have lost jobs, so chances are that you know someone who has a similar experience as you. You can talk about how your friends' families coped with their job losses, what advice they have, and how they felt at the time.

How Your Parents Feel

No matter how bad you feel about your parent losing his or her job, remember that the rest of your family is suffering too. Be especially sensitive to the parent who actually lost a job. He or she is probably pretty upset, even though staying home all day and watching TV sounds much better to you than going to work and sitting in an office. Be patient with your parents, if they yell at you more often than usual, or if they seem sad and tired a lot. They have a lot to think about and a lot to worry about, and they need some time to figure out what they should do about the job loss.

Your Mom and Dad are probably experiencing some difficult emotions, too, as they try to pay all the bills and keep the family going.

Even though your family is going through a hard time right now, you will still be able to have fun together sometimes. And things will get better.

The Future

It won't always be so confusing. If your mom or dad looks hard, chances are good a new job will come along eventually. Or your dad will get a promotion at his job, and your mom won't have to look for work anymore, if she doesn't want to. Something will work out! In the meantime, your family will be eligible for unemployment insurance, which is money the government pays to people who have lost their jobs.

Whatever happens, you'll get used to your new routine soon enough. It might be strange to have your mom or dad at home now, or it may take some time to get used to living in a new town, but it'll feel normal before you know it. Life always involves change—but it works out in the end!

Questions to Think About

1. How do you think Kayley will feel if she has to move to a new town?

2. What other things might Kayley have had to give up after her dad lost his job?

3. What would you do if one of your parents lost their job?

4. What were some of the emotions that Kayley's parents were going through?

Further Reading

Alpern, Michele, and Marvin Rosen. *The Effects of Job Loss on the Family.* New York: Chelsea House, 2002.

Berg, Adriane, and Arthur Berg Bochner. *The Totally Awesome Money Book for Kids, Second Edition.* New York: Newmarket Press, 2002.

Croke, Liam. *I'm Broke! The Money Handbook.* New York: Crabtree Publishing, 2009.

Idle, Molly Schaar. *Head's Up: A Story of One Quarter.* Nashville, Tenn.: Abingdon Press, 2004.

Find Out More on the Internet

Families Handling the Recession
p b s k i d s . o r g / i t s m y l i f e / f a m i l y / y o u _ s a i d _
it.html?ysiTitle = handling_recession

How to Explain Being Unemployed to Children
jobmob.co.il/blog/family-unemployment/

Talking to Kids About Layoffs
life.familyeducation.com/money-management/work/61368.
html

Unemployment in the Family
w w w . c y h . c o m / H e a l t h T o p i c s / H e a l t h T o p i c D e t a i l s K i d s .
aspx?p = 335&np = 282&id = 1583

When Parents Lose a Job
life.familyeducation.com/money-and-kids/communica-
tion/29623.html

Index

Picture Credits

AVAVA, fotolia: p. 30
Creative Commons Attribution 2.0 Generic
   Metro Centric: p. 29
Fouveure, Hervé; fotolia: p. 42

Ghost, fotolia: p. 41
nyul, fotolia: p. 27
Rob, fotolia: p. 38
sparkmom, fotolia: p. 37
Yamashita, Karl; fotolia: p. 34

To the best knowledge of the publisher, all images not specifically credited are in the public domain. If any image has been inadvertently uncredited, please notify Harding House Publishing Service, 220 Front Street, Vestal, New York 13850, so that credit can be given in future printings.

About the Authors

Sheila Stewart has written several dozen books for young people, both fiction and nonfiction, although she especially enjoys writing fiction. She has a master's degree in English and now works as a writer and editor. She lives with her two children in a house overflowing with books, in the Southern Tier of New York State.

Rae Simons is a freelance author who has written numerous educational books for children and young adults. She also has degrees in psychology and special education, and she has worked with children encountering a range of troubles in their lives.

About the Consultant

Cindy Croft, M.A. Ed., is Director of the Center for Inclusive Child Care, a state-funded program with support from the McKnight Foundation, that creates, promotes, and supports pathways to successful inclusive care for all children. Its goal is inclusion and retention of children with disabilities and behavioral challenges in community child care settings. Cindy Croft is also on the faculty at Concordia University, where she teaches courses on young children with special needs and the emotional growth of young children. She is the author of several books, including *The Six Keys: Strategies for Promoting Children's Mental Health*.